A Pocketful of
Bible Stories

A LION BOOK

Text copyright © 1979 and 1980 Lion Publishing
Illustrations copyright © 1979 and 1980 Graham Round

Published by
Lion Publishing plc
Sandy Lane West, Oxford, England
ISBN 0 7459 3059 X
Lion Publishing
4050 Lee Vance View, Colorado Springs, CO 80918, USA
ISBN 0 7459 3059 X
Albatross Books Pty Ltd
PO Box 320, Sutherland, NSW 2232, Australia
ISBN 0 7324 1201 3

This edition first published in 1995
10 9 8 7 6 5 4 3 2 1

A catalogue record for this book
is available from the British Library

Library of Congress CIP Data applied for

Printed in Singapore

Miriam and the Princess

A story from the Old Testament
retold by Philip Henderson

Pictures by Graham Round

This is a story from long ago, seventeen hundred years before Jesus was born. God's people, the Israelites, were living in Egypt. They were slaves.

All day long they worked in the hot sun making bricks to build new palaces for the king.

But God had a plan for his people. He was going to set them free.

And this is how it all began. . .

In a house near the River Nile in Egypt lived a little Israelite girl called Miriam.

Miriam's father was a slave, like all the Israelites.
It was very hard work, and he was tired and sad.

But Miriam was happy and excited. Her mother was going to have a baby.

"Will it be a boy or a girl?" she asked her father.
"I want a baby brother."

"It must not be a boy," he said. "The Egyptians have orders to kill every Israelite baby boy."

At last the baby was born. And it was a boy.

"We can't let the Egyptians kill our baby," cried Miriam's mother. "God can't want that to happen."

So they decided to hide the baby. Miriam looked after him, and made sure he didn't cry.

But, all the time, the baby was getting bigger.
Soon everyone nearby knew he was there.

"Miriam," her mother said, "I have a plan
to keep our baby alive. And you can help me."

They took the baby's basket and made a lid for it.
They painted it with tar to keep any water out.

Early next morning they went down to the river, where the Princess of Egypt swam every day.

They hid the basket boat amongst the reeds. Safe inside, fast asleep, was Miriam's baby brother!

Then Miriam hid and waited. At last the princess came to the river for her morning swim.

"Oh look!" cried the princess. "A little boat!
And there's something in it!"

She opened the lid, and the baby began to cry.

"What a lovely baby," the princess said. "He must be an Israelite. I shall make him my own son."

The plan had worked! Miriam was so excited that she ran up to the princess.

"Your highness," said Miriam, "let me find a nurse to look after the baby for you."

"Thank you," said the princess. So Miriam ran
off to fetch the baby's own mother!

The princess was very pleased. "Take care of the baby for me," she said, "and I will pay you well."

"When he is old enough he must come to the palace to be my son. I shall call him Moses."

So Miriam and her mother took Moses back home and looked after him. How happy they all were.

"God has been very good to us," said Miriam's father. "He must have a great plan for you, Moses."

And Miriam's father was right.
For God had chosen Moses to free
his people from the Egyptians.
But that is another story . . .

You can read this story in your Bible,
in Exodus chapter 2.

Elijah and the Great Drought

A story from the Old Testament
retold by Philip Henderson

Pictures by Graham Round

This is a story from long ago, eight hundred years before Jesus was born. God's people, the Israelites, were ruled by a wicked king, called Ahab. He had done so many wrong things that he had to be punished.
But God still cared for the people of Israel.

King Ahab was wicked and cruel.

One day Elijah the prophet came to him with a message.

"God says, 'If you don't stop being wicked,
I will stop sending the rain.'"

But King Ahab would not listen. There was no rain that day. Or the next. Or the next.

Elijah went to a secret place by a stream.
And still there was no rain.

Soon the rivers dried up. The grass withered
and the sheep grew hungry and thin and died.

The crops would not grow, and there was no bread to eat.

For two long years there was no rain.
At last there was no food left.

Then God told Elijah to leave his secret place,
and set off for the little town of Zarephath.

In Zarephath lived a poor widow with her son.

All they had left to eat was a handful of flour
and a few drops of oil.

"This will be our last meal," said the widow.
"Then we shall have to go hungry."

The widow went out to fetch wood to cook the meal. While she was busy, a stranger came up to her.

It was Elijah. "Please give me a drink of water,"
he said. "I have come a long way to see you."

"And I'd like some bread, too," Elijah called after her.

"I have no bread to give you," said the woman.
"I am cooking one last meal for my son and myself."

"Don't worry," said Elijah. "God has promised to look after you."

"Go and get your meal ready, but make me a small loaf first."

The widow did not know what to say. She hurried home and called her son.

"Elijah the prophet has come to our house.
We must share our last meal with him."

When she had baked the loaf, she gave it to Elijah.
"Go on," he said. "Now make yourself some food."

The widow picked up the jars. She could hardly believe her eyes. They were not empty after all!

There was plenty of oil and flour! That day the widow and her son ate till they were full.

"God is looking after us," said Elijah. "He will not let the food run out until the rain comes."

And Elijah was right.
The jars were never empty again,
however much the widow took
from them.
Elijah stayed with the widow and
her son for many days, until the time
came when God sent the rain again.
But that is another story . . .

You can find this story in your Bible,
in 1 Kings chapter 17.

Naaman and the Servant Girl

A story from the Old Testament
retold by Philip Henderson

This is a story from long ago, eight
hundred years before Jesus was born.
God's people, the Israelites, were
at war with the Syrians.
The Israelites were often beaten,
but God always looked after them.

Naaman the Syrian was a very great general.

His army always beat the Israelites, God's people.

After one raid, Naaman captured a little Israelite girl and took her back to Syria to be his servant.

She had to wash the clothes and clean the house and cook the meals. It was hard work.

Naaman was very rich and famous. He had lots of friends.

But one day, Naaman looked in the mirror and had a terrible shock.

His face was covered with white blotches.

Every day the illness got worse. Even the best doctor in Syria could not help him.

Soon people ran away when they saw Naaman.
"I can never lead the army again," he said.

No one knew what to do—except for the little
servant girl from Israel.

"God can make you better," she said. "Go to Israel and ask Elisha. He will tell you what to do."

So Naaman set off. He took his servants, and bags of gold and silver to pay Elisha the prophet.

It was a long, long journey from Syria to Israel but at last they came to Elisha's house.

Naaman knocked at the door, but no one came out to answer.

At last Elisha sent his servant with a message:
"Go and wash in the River Jordan! Seven times!"

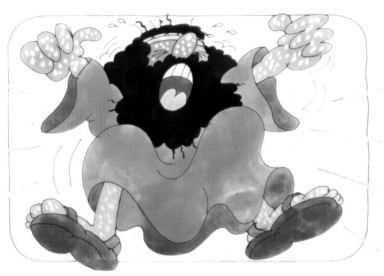

Naaman was very angry. "I haven't come all this
way to wash in your filthy river!" he shouted.

But his servant said, "Sir, you ought to try.
It might make you better."

"All right," said Naaman, "I will." So down
he went to the River Jordan, and in he jumped . . .

SPLOOSH!

SPLASH!

SPLOSH!

SPLASH!

SPERLOOSHHHHHH!!

"I'm better!" he shouted. "The blotches have all gone!"

So Naaman ran all the way back to Elisha's house,
to give him a thank you present.

But Elisha would not take Naaman's present. "It's God who has made you better, not me," he said.

Naaman could hardly believe it. The God of Israel loved even the enemies of his people.

When Naaman got back to Syria, there
was a big party.
And the first person to meet him
was the little servant girl.
"Hooray, hooray!" she shouted.
"I knew God would make you well.
He loves and cares for everyone
in the whole wide world."

You can find this story in your Bible,
in 2 Kings chapter 5.

Nehemiah Builds a City

A story from the Old Testament
retold by Philip Henderson

Pictures by Graham Round

This is a story from long ago, six hundred years before Jesus was born. The Babylonian army had captured Jerusalem. They had taken away God's people, the Jews, to far-off Babylonia. For seventy long years the Jews lived there, a long, long way from home. Then Babylon itself was captured and the new emperor let the Jews go home to Jerusalem.

But some of them stayed on . . .

Nehemiah was a very important man in Babylon.
He brought the emperor his wine at dinner.

But Nehemiah's home was in Jerusalem, far away.
One day, a letter came from his brother there.

"Jerusalem is in ruins," said the letter. "Our enemies, Sanballat and Tobiah, are laughing at us."

Nehemiah was very sad when he heard this news.
He asked God to show him what to do.

Then one day, when Nehemiah was serving the wine, the emperor asked him why he looked so sad.

"How can I help it," Nehemiah said. "God's city is in ruins. Please let me go and build it again."

"Very well," said the emperor. "You can go
and I will give you all the wood you need."

Nehemiah could hardly believe his ears.
"Now I know God will help me," he said.

Sanballat and Tobiah heard the news. They were angry. "He must not build up the walls," they said.

When Nehemiah reached Jerusalem, all his friends met him. But he did not tell them about his plan.

He waited until it was dark. Then he set off on his donkey to inspect the city.

The walls were broken down and the gates had been burnt. It was a terrible sight.

Next morning, Nehemiah held a meeting. "We must build the walls again," he said. "God will help us."

Everyone agreed. "Let's start now," they shouted.
"Let's build God's city together."

For days and days they worked. Some carried
stones, and others built the walls.

Some cut wood, and others built the gates.
Every day the walls grew higher and higher.

But Sanballat and Tobiah were plotting.
"Let's try to make them feel silly," they said.

"Even a fox could knock down those feeble walls,"
they shouted. But Nehemiah took no notice.

So Sanballat and Tobiah made a new plan.
"Let's break in and wreck the gates," they said.

They waited until it was dark. Then they crept up to attack the city.

But Nehemiah was ready for them. His guards drove them back.

"You can't frighten us," Nehemiah shouted.
"This is God's work, and he will look after us."

And Nehemiah was right. The work went on
and soon the walls were finished.

"God has helped us build the walls," said
Nehemiah. "Now our city is safe to live in."

The priests blew their trumpets and everyone marched along the top of the wall, thanking God and singing.

After that they had a party that lasted a whole week!

Nehemiah became the city governor —the best they ever had.

You can find this story in your Bible.
It is in the book called Nehemiah.

The Lost Sheep

A parable of Jesus
retold by Meryl Doney

Pictures by Graham Round

One day Jesus' friends asked him:
"Who does God love most?"
"My father loves everyone," said Jesus.
He pointed to a little child.
"Children are not big and strong. They
trust their parents to look after them.
My father wants people to trust him
and love him just like that. He will look
after them."
"What if they go away from God, and
don't love him?" asked one of Jesus'
friends.
So Jesus told this story . . .

Once upon a time, there was a shepherd who had a hundred sheep.

He looked after them. He found them grass to eat and water to drink.

At night he led them safely home to their sheep-pen.

The shepherd counted them as they went in through the gate.

One night he counted and there were only ninety-nine sheep.

One sheep was lost. The shepherd was very worried.

He set off straight away to look for the sheep.

He took with him his shepherd's stick and a bag of food.

He called to the sheep as he walked. Soon it was dark.

But still the shepherd searched among the rocks and prickly bushes.

Suddenly, the shepherd heard a feeble bleat.
It was his sheep crying.

He ran towards the sound.

There was his sheep, caught in the bushes!

He used his shepherd's stick to get her out. Then he took her in his arms.

He carried her back to the sheep-pen on his shoulders.

The ninety-nine sheep were safe inside, waiting for him.

Gently the shepherd put his lost sheep down with the others.

She was so glad to be back home. She skipped
and jumped for joy.

The shepherd was glad, too. He hurried to tell all his friends.

"I have found my lost sheep. I am going to have a party," he said.

Some brought pipes and drums to make music.
Others sang and danced.

It was a wonderful party.

Everyone was glad the sheep had been found.

. . . and she was glad to be safe home again, too.

"My father is like that shepherd," said Jesus. "He knows us all by name. If one of us goes away from him, he will come to look for us, because he loves us. When he brings us back, he is as glad as the shepherd in my story."

You can find this story in your Bible,
in Matthew chapter 18.

The Two Houses

A parable of Jesus
retold by Meryl Doney

Pictures by Graham Round

One day, Jesus was teaching his friends.
Some listened hard. But others were not
really listening at all. Jesus said to them:
"If you trust God and do what he wants,
you will be safe and happy. You will be
like the man who built his house on a rock."
Then he began to tell them this story . . .

Once upon a time, there were two men. Each wanted to build himself a house.

They counted their money. Then they looked for a good place to build.

The first man was in hurry. ''I want my house now,'' he said.

He found a sandy place. "This is a nice flat place
to build my house!" he said.

Soon the house was finished. Everyone came to look at it.

"What a beautiful house you've built," they said.

The second man thought about his house.
"I want to build my house safe and strong," he said.
"Then it will last."

He found a place where there was rock. "If I build on the rock my house will be safe," he thought.

His house took a long time. But when it was finished, everyone came to look at it.

"What a beautiful house you've built,' they said.

The two men lived happily in their houses.

But one day dark clouds rolled across the sky.

"A great storm is coming," everyone said.

The storm came. The wind blew and the rain fell on the two houses.

The first man looked out at the storm. "I hope my house is safe," he said.

But it was only built on sand. His house shook, and creaked and . . .

CRASH—it fell down flat. The sand was not strong enough to hold it.

Every little bit was blown away in the storm.

The second man also looked out at the storm.
"I'm sure my house is safe," he said.

His house was built on the strong rock.

It shook, and it creaked, but it DID NOT FALL.

It stood safe and strong until the storm had gone.

The second man was safe and happy in his
strong house.

But no one knows what happened to the first man.

"Listen," said Jesus. "People who do not trust God and do what he wants are like the first man, who built his house on sand. But people who trust God and do what he wants are like the second man. He knew he was building to last, on the strong rock. People like him are safe and happy whatever happens."

You can find this story in your Bible,
in Luke chapter 6.

The Loving Father

A parable of Jesus
retold by Meryl Doney

Pictures by Graham Round

Jesus had many friends who were not
good people. He loved them all.
But the good people did not like this.
"How can he love these bad people?"
they said to themselves. "God only loves
good people."
Jesus heard them. "God loves everyone,"
he said. "He wants to forgive people who
have been bad. He can help them to be good."
His friends said, "Tell us what God is like."
So Jesus told them this story . . .

Once upon a time, there was a rich man who had two sons.

He promised to give his money to his sons when he died.

The elder son was good. He said, "I'll stay at home
to help, father."

But the younger son did not want to help his father.

"Please give me my share of the money now," he said. "I want to go away and enjoy myself."

So he took his money, and left home. His father was very sad.

The younger son went off to the big city. He had a
wonderful time.

He bought a grand house and beautiful clothes
and a horse to ride.

He had lots of friends. He invited them to parties at his house.

Soon all his money was gone.

So he sold his house, his horse and even his
beautiful clothes.

His friends all left him. Before long he had no food left to eat.

He had to take a job looking after pigs. He was so hungry he even ate their food.

Then he remembered his father and his home.

"I have done all the wrong things," he said to himself. "Will my father forgive me?"

"I will go home," he decided. "Perhaps he will let me be a servant."

So he set off on the long journey home. He
walked all the way.

At last, he saw his home. There was someone
outside . . .

It was his father. He ran to meet his son because he was so glad to see him. He still loved him very much.

"Father I have been very wrong," said the son.
"Will you forgive me?"

"Yes," said his father. "I have waited every day for you to come home."

"Bring him new clothes, and a ring," he called.
"Get ready for a party!"

"My son is sorry for all he has done. I have forgiven him. I am so happy."

They had a wonderful party. Everyone danced and sang for joy.

"God is like that father," said Jesus.
"He wants people to come and say they are sorry for being bad. Then he will forgive them and help them to be good. When that happens, he is very happy, just like the father in my story."

You can find this story in your Bible,
in Luke chapter 15.

The Kind Stranger

A parable of Jesus,
retold by Meryl Doney

Pictures by Graham Round

One day a young man came to Jesus.
He was a good man. But he was very proud.
 He thought he knew everything.
"Teacher," he said. "How can I please God?"
"What do you think?" asked Jesus.
"By loving God and helping people,"
answered the man.
"Yes," said Jesus.
"Which people should I help?" asked the man.
So Jesus told him this story . . .

Once upon a time, a man set out on a journey.
The road was very lonely.

It was just the place for robbers. The man looked round anxiously.

Suddenly some robbers jumped out from behind the rocks.

They hit the man on the head. He fell off
his donkey.

They beat him up and snatched his purse.

Then they ran away, leaving him by the roadside.

The man lay still. His head hurt. He could not shout for help.

Then he saw someone coming along the road.

"At last!" he thought. "Here's someone who will help me."

But the man was in a hurry. He did not stop to help.

The burning sun shone down. The man who had
been robbed felt very ill.

Suddenly he saw another man coming along the road. "He will be sure to help me," he thought.

But this was an important man. He was in a hurry too.

He looked at the injured man, but he did not stop to help him.

Hours passed: the sun was going down. The man felt very ill indeed.

Then, along came another person. He was a Samaritan, from the land of Samaria.

(People in Jesus' country didn't like Samaritans in those days.)

When this Samaritan saw the man, he stopped to help him at once.

He got off his donkey and gave him a drink.

He cleaned and bandaged his cuts. Then he put him on his own donkey.

They both set off up the road to find a place to stay for the night.

When they arrived at the nearest inn, the Samaritan put the man to bed.

The Samaritan asked the innkeeper to look after
the man.

"I will pay you for everything," he said. The next day he rode off on his donkey.

"Now," said Jesus to the young man,
"which of those three people really helped
the injured man?"
"The Samaritan," said the young man.
"Then go and do the same," smiled Jesus.
"Help anyone who needs help. That is what
pleases God."

You can find this story in your Bible,
in Luke chapter 10.